Letters to a Devastated Christian

Letters to a Devastated Christian

By Gene Edwards

CHRISTIAN BOOKS
Auburn, Maine

ISBN 0-940232-13-8

CHRISTIAN BOOKS
P.O. Box 3368
Auburn, Maine 04210

Dedication

To Barbara Kloos, the lovely lady who managed Christian Books for several years, and who championed the production of this book even before it was written.

Acknowledgement

To the hundreds of Christians who have written me for help in their search to shake off a shipwrecked condition, to find again the Polar Star of their faith and return once more to the Christian quest.

Author's Note

If anyone ever uses these letters to try to bring harm to any group or movement it will be over my protest. I've seen some pretty hair-raising Sauls in my life, but I've met some Absaloms as bad or worse. There is not a group, nor movement, nor simple house meeting but what *A Tale of Three Kings* (and these letters) could be used against it. Written in Hebrew, these two pieces of literature could have been used against Simon Peter 2,000 years ago. Or Paul. I have problems with men making such use of another man's words. And I put in deep suspect any man—anywhere—that sows discord with *any* movement. Period. No matter how gross that work might *appear* to him.

1

Dear Ken:

You asked me what I know of "Discipleship," "Authoritarianism," "Shepherdism," and/or "Hyper-eldering."

Well, I could accurately answer that without knowing anything about *any* authoritarian movement that has arisen in the last 200 years. The basic characteristics have been here from the church's most primitive times; authoritarian oppression seems to be a genetic thing inherent to man. I am certain authoritarian movements will surface again and again throughout future generations just as they have in the past. And there will be followers aplenty to respond, I hasten to add.

Historically this concept began outside—and before—Christendom. The Romans had the custom of placing a clenched fist over the heart and proclaiming something to the effect of, "For Rome." The sense conveyed was, "There is something we are part of that is greater than we are and, at all cost, it comes first." The idea was so all-pervading that no one questioned what the *something* was.. though a poll might have turned up the information that no one really knew.

The Roman Catholic church became the recipient, inheritor, incubator and promulgator of this Roman mindframe. Every human being who lived in Europe lived in an all-encompassing environment that said, "You give allegiance to the mother church."

On what basis? On no other basis than the fact that, if you breathed and lived in Europe, the church was your unquestioned mother.

Other movements that have followed the Roman Catholic church have created this same scenario. Some wittingly, some unwittingly. Some movements were secular, some political, and some religious. We who walk the religious arena are the most susceptible because somehow we get the idea that the all-encompassing *something* we are caught up in may be of God... maybe even His central purpose... and because we love Him we sincerely wish to please Him; and if we don't go along with this *something*, we may displease Him.

Oh, and another reason! We fallen creatures love to think we are *it:* "*I* am in *the* movement."

Long before this century came along, the characteristics of authoritarian Christian movements were set. Let's look at some of the most frequently found attributes stressed among authoritarian groups of Christians, be they evangelicals, high church protestants, Catholics, or any other species of Christendom's menagerie.

SPECIALISM:

"We are special." "We are the only group..." Or: "We are not the only group, but we are a very *special* group in God's eyes." Or: "We are the cutting edge of God's work in this generation." Or worse: "There is nobody except *us* who has the truth."

You might think I've just described the motto of the group with whom you have been associated. Not at all. I have just described many of church history's most famous movements. Either presently, or some time in the past, many—if not most—have held this view. (Some groups state these ideas straight out. Others only imply them... the latter approach being every bit as effective.) Who? Catholics, Lutherans, Church of England, Presbyterians, Quakers,

Baptists, Methodists, Moravians, Waldensians, Plymouth Brethren, Pentecostals, ad infinitum. All these movements have at one time or another presented themselves as the one *true* movement. I am prepared to believe it is impossible—based on the facts of church history—to draw a large number of people to a Christian movement unless this "we are it" attitude is introduced and avidly promulgated.

"Specialism" is an accepted, yet rarely verbalized, tool of the trade. You'll look hard to find a Christian group that has never employed this tool.

Ken, the truth is not far from this statement: Some of the most powerful, earth-shaking, history-changing movements in the annals of our faith drew their awesome power not so much from the power of the Holy Spirit as from the enthusiasm, sweat, and sacrifice of idealistic young people caught up in the dream that they were God's chosen work of that age. Vision plus sweat have done a lot more in church history than brokenness and humility have ever done.

Rare, rarer, rarest is the man or the movement that does not make hay with this tool. Name the men and movements who have impelled men solely by introducing them to the daily encounters of the riches of Jesus Christ, please. It's a very short list. And why do more men not impel Christians by flooding them with Christ? Why so much dependence on "specialism"? The answer is obvious. Men can't give away an abundance of that which they themselves have only in short supply.

Unfortunately, this state of affairs will continue if we can judge any of the future by all of the past. "Specialism" will be part and parcel of future movements if for no other reason than inexperienced young people believe that the small morsel their leaders are giving them is an unprecedented feast. They conclude, therefore, the movement they are in must be "it" because it has so much light and life, not realizing that most of what they are getting is borrowed, *something old*.

Let us hope that one day there arrives on the scene honest men who will not traffic in these counterfeited goods . . . and who will dispense Christ. Christ, with no "movement" salesmanship added in. And let's hope those men have Him... in abundance. Broken men are needed; men—and women—with no ax to grind, no movement to trade in, but Christ alone as their center and circumference. Also needed are a people who will respond with all their hearts and souls, without exclusiveness being part of what motivates them.

I add one word. Head for the door when a man or a people declare: "We are the work of God for this generation." Mind you, there are groups that *are* God's work in virtually every age. But no one, repeat, *no one* knows *which* work that is. Years later, in retrospect, history will declare it... but that comes at least 100 years later. In our own lifetimes we simply cannot know! The man who declares the movement that *he* is in to be *the* work of God in his generation is either a fake, a fortune teller, or... oh well.

The second most frequently found ingredient in authoritarian movements in *any age* is the call to oneness in the body of Christ:

THE NEED FOR UNITY IN THE BODY OF CHRIST:

In a way, this idea is brand new. In another, it is one of the oldest tools employed by the hidden hearts of men.

The Catholics held the western world together with the concept of unity for well over a thousand years. Some potent idea this! Who can fault it? I cannot. Unity in Christ's body must surely be the dream even of angels. Unfortunately, I cannot recall ever encountering any sizeable group that employed this appeal with pure motives. The Roman Catholics, for instance, used torture chambers to "keep the unity" of the body of Christ.

Today, this tool is being overworked, especially by some of the movements—I am grieved to say—who are outside the religious system. Using the theme of unity to build a movement is a sad spectacle to watch. Of all places purity of motive in the matter of unity should be, it should be among Christians who are outside formalized Christianity.

In the last few years, the methods and skulduggery used under the guise of unity have become a science. It goes like this:

Taking the prayer of Christ to the Father, a Christian worker begins calling for unity in the body of Christ. Each time he—or his group—stumbles upon a little band of Christians struggling along in their small meetings, the worker begins to meet with them and speaks to them on the unity of the body of Christ "in these last days." The struggling little group responds to this call and joins the larger movement. The idea is oneness in all the body of Christ. In practice though, this is but a *method,* growth by absorption.[1] Others in this movement catch on to this effective, yet undeclared, approach to growth. They start doing the same thing. Soon one of the highest hopes of the Christian heart—unity in the body of Christ—is reduced to nothing but a dubious method to increase the size of the movement. I might add that any men who use that method in order to increase the size of their movement are— perhaps unknowingly—undercutting their conscience and taking a giant step toward learning *Christian worker dishonesty.*

Frankly, I have a much higher regard for the out and out sheep stealer than the worker who courts other groups in a call for unity. A Scriptural case *can* be built for justifying outright sheep stealing, you know. (See Paul turned loose in a synagogue!) A left-handed call for unity in the body of Christ is somehow taking advantage of a thing too dear to all our hearts for what is really only a thinly disguised method for numerical growth.

One last observation. An unusually large emphasis on unity accomplishes two things dear to most any worker, though he may not necessarily mention them. First, a call to unity keeps down trouble and dissension. (No one wants to bring disunity to the church.) Second, it keeps up membership. (To leave is to divide the body.) People are afraid to "break the unity."

As I said, this is some potent tool. To sum up, in this generation, beware the worker bearing an inordinate dose of unity.

THE NEED OF A CHRISTIAN GROUP
TO HAVE HEAD COVERING:

This call is the twin brother of the one just mentioned. Instead of calling for unity, the worker approaches a struggling, independent little group of Christians on the grounds that "all men need to be covered."

"God's people in this group need to be covered by local elders...but the elders need to be covered too. They need to be covered by _____." (What word fits in this blank? Bishops? Apostles? Overshepherds? Pastors? Workers? It depends on the vocabulary of the particular movement.)

"Those at the top," he tells us, "are covered by Christ, and Christ is covered by God."

If you think this is something new under the sun, you underestimate the ancients in being as sagacious as modern men in thinking up schemes to increase membership, preserve unity, keep down problems and in general scare the wits out of us. This concept is as old as Roman Catholicism's centuries-old call to return to the Mother Church, the Pope and the Cardinals. And such a call works. Amazingly. Groups as divergent as Roman Popes, all the way over to Christian workers who are outside the religious system, use this same unscrupulous and unscriptural method to preserve a movement's unity.

These three ingredients—Specialism, Unity, Head Covering over churches—go together to make up a large part of the stew called "authoritarianism."[2] You need only a solemn elders meeting or message delivered on the Scripture teachings of "*submission* to divine authority" and you have something as new as the present-day authoritarian movement and as old as that much feared decree, the papal bull.

2

Dear Ken:

Why has authoritarianism raised its familiar head periodically throughout church history? Just because "it is Scriptural"? Unlikely. So, too, are a myriad other things "Scriptural" that aren't nearly so recurringly popular. The answer must be somewhere else.

(Having spent my entire adult life in the Christian ministry and being a student both of history and the passing parade, I am prepared to believe that no event has ever taken place in church history but what someone was present who could prove beyond doubt that whatever the grisly thing they were doing—be it murdering, torturing or maiming—it was being done squarely on Scriptural teachings. Anything, everything, seems to be not only Scripturally provable . . . but Scripturally central! Poor God. Whatever shall He do with us mortals?)

It is my studied judgment that there has never been a revival of any peripheral doctrine but what there was first some other reason besides Scripture that provoked rolling out the old thing and dressing it up in new clothes. I just as firmly believe that inordinate emphasis on a doctrine finds its true birth first, not in Scripture, but in the unspoken and hidden motives of the heart of the Christian worker who is pushing it so hard.

To the point: the present authoritarian emphasis was probably born out of men fearing division in their movement. The reason for that fear was probably well founded: memories of the past failures in their ministry caused by division.

Fear. Fear that the ensuing chaos coming from the division would cause their work—their movement—to fail.

So, with vivid memories of past divisions and ugly clashes, with the specter of past problems stalking them, Christian workers turned to dictatorship in the name of Scripture to thereby build a work void of major disunities. Nonetheless, I doubt that any man would ever allow himself to know he embraced authoritarianism for this reason. Surely, he would never so state himself publicly. (These are things the mind is never allowed to hear, but the heart knows too well. The heart rarely tells the mind what it is doing, or why it is doing the things it does.)

Oh, by the way, ere you grab this letter and run door-to-door to your friends crying, "I've got the goods. I've got the goods," you had best know that men who run door-to-door to stir up trouble against a worker are no better in heart motive than the worker who (they perceive) needs exposing.

Perhaps we will speak more to that subject later.

3

Dear Ken:

I've been reflecting on your question, "Could you assess the result of the damage that has come out of the present authoritarian movement?" That's a rather tall order; the damage has been so wide-spread and downright awesome. Here are a few impressions, nonetheless, that float to the surface.

- Young men and young women learned how to rebuke and criticize one another when they were in an authoritarian movement. This is something no one should learn well. Sometimes rebuke gets to be an almost savage thing. Christians, especially young ones, ought not to do such things to one another.
- Pride in people's hearts was appealed to, cultivated, watered and fertilized.
- Men and women who left those movements lost all hope in even the theoretical honesty of Christian workers. That is doubly tragic. If you lose trust in Christians, you have absolutely nowhere to go.
- Families divided—splits, separations, divorces.
- Christians lost—or never got a chance to lay hold of—the won-

drous, unshackling experience of *liberty in Christ*.

- Fear and confusion became the order of the day.
- Young men and young women who might have grown up—and grown old—serving the Lord as workers were ruined...forever.
- Across our land have grown up little pockets of Christians who are bitter and shipwrecked. They seem to be able to find one another, move near one another, and fraternize together—like glazed-eyed beings in Dante's Inferno—forever dining on nightmares, partaking of mutual cynicism and hopelessness. *That* is the saddest of all scenes.

(There is no cause for a Christian to be *that* wrecked. No. No justification for it whatsoever.)

I have been struck by not only the above scene, but by the opposite. I have looked at the leaders of the movements that have presided over this carnage and wondered if they are not aware of the thousands of shipwrecked lives out there. There appears to be an almost total disregard—by the leaders in these groups—of the mounting and appalling destruction resulting from authoritarianism.

But I wish to be just as quick to say, "Can the 'outs' not grasp what *their* conduct looks like? Their deep, ever nurtured hurts are as indefensible as are the 'ins' who traffic in authoritarianism destruction."

I have been subjected to barnfuls of stories about authoritarianism and I feel very uncomfortable about everything I hear...from either side.

I recall, a few years ago, there must have been several thousand home groups meeting across western America. There was no form, little ritual, and there was *freedom* by the bushel in these neat little gatherings. To the last one, all these very free little groups collapsed and folded. As a result of this wholesale collapse, authoritarianism entered and flourished. Now, a decade has passed. The free home meeting groups are not only dead, but totally forgotten, and the authoritarianism concept that took their place is experiencing an awesome reaction. Why?

Remember those bright-eyed, idealistic, very gullible and

wonderful Christian kids of ten years ago? Now they have reached their inevitable 30-34 year-old stage where a life crisis awaits all of them. They are reacting. Trouble is everywhere. It was inevitable. At 20 you'll believe almost anything. At 32 you are grown up and can get pretty upset about having been misused in your more gullible years. Some of these older Christians are bound to react. Lines are drawn; names are called. The battle begins and only carnage follows.

Listen to the few survivors of authoritarianism when they get together. Listen to them talk about what went wrong, what they now believe the church should be like—based on their bad experiences. Some feel strongly that "total freedom" is the only way the church should meet. (No elders. No nothing.) This is a reaction to all things smacking of leadership . . . like someone announcing there is going to be a meeting! On the other extreme, some men think there should be no Christian gathering unless there are supervisors present to watchdog every move. Both views are nothing more than reactions, having little to do with Scripture or with the Spirit of Christ, and a lot to do with past bad experiences.

Viewing things from these two vantage points, I can only say this whole tragedy of the last few years is taking on the attributes of a vast holocaust.

The problem with men running other Christians' lives—or counterwise, the idea of freedom so utter that it throws out gatherings—is *not* the issue. The problem is much more simple than that.

A move of the Lord's spirit began ten or fifteen years ago in our land. No one who got caught up in that movement was equal to the demands. The thing was doomed from the outset, Ken. Proper men did not exist. The men who did step forth to become leaders were unbroken men with a fuzzy view of Christ, of His church, and of His ways. Those who followed those unqualified men got thrown into—or appointed to—positions which they, too, were not qualified to handle. Using some of the most gosh-awful methods conceivable, the whole thing seems, today, to be ending in shambles.

Furthermore, I shudder to think what would happen if the

Lord's spirit again blew across our land. There are few qualified men abroad in this country who can lead a new generation of young hearts. (I make that statement unequivocably.) If a new breath blew across our land, if a new work started today and it had to be led by men who are available today, I have a notion that 15 years from now you would see just as much carnage. And that carnage would occur even if authoritarianism was never introduced.

The problem was not doctrine nor practice. The problem was hearts.

I see a comical side to such a scenario, too. If a new breath of God blew today, and little groups and little works began popping up across our land, I see in my mind's eye delegates from both sides of the present authoritarian issue coming around these new groups saying to them either, "Don't have elders. Don't have elders." Or "Freedom won't work. Freedom won't work."

Is there any hope? I think so, but a little humility on the part of those of us who are workers could sure go a long way.

The order of the day ought to be: We are not first century. We have no physical Jesus Christ who tutored twelve of us for three years. Pentecost did not happen nine years ago. We who are workers today, without exception, were born and lived in Babylon (or served under men with the ways of Babylon dripping from their garments). If we arrogantly try for a "do it all in one generation" leap back to the ways of the primeval church...we will fail. We, living today, simply are not that qualified to do a pure work. None of us. And one adult lifetime is not long enough to resolve the problems we face. Why are men so arrogant as to think themselves special enough to do this whole task of restoration in twenty years? The best we workers can possibly do is shield a group of young men and women from the present-day Christendom's corruption, give them a positive environment to grow in, point them to the deep things of Christ, give them church life at the best it can now be experienced (which isn't far), and press them *beyond* our spiritual growth and our limits in Christ. Then hope. Hope these kids, when grown, will best all of us. Hope that they will reach for the stars. Hope that they will pass on to the next generation an experience of

Christ—and His church—higher than anything the last generation has known or can know.

What am I saying? That we are not qualified, in one generation, to make the necessary leap to restore things needing restoration.[3]

In the meantime, I would encourage you to stop licking your wounds and stop reacting against "authoritarianism." It was not authoritarianism that did you in. It was a second-rate approach to restoration by men not quite up to the job...plus your very willing decision to join up. Ken, had they taken some other tack besides authoritarianism, that would have failed just as perfectly. Your generation bit off more than it could chew. This present scene of chaos and carnage was inevitable. Let us pray for a future that contains better days and better men, higher motivations on the part of those who proclaim and those who respond.

4

Dear Ken:

There is one type of damage being experienced among Christians who have pulled out of authoritarian groups that is, perhaps, the most tragic of all. In listening, I get the deep impression that many saints have left the Lord. (No, that's not it. Rather, they fear that the Lord has left them.) A Christian who has joined a really wonderful, dynamic, and yes, God-blessed movement, who has heard messages few Christians have heard, experienced what few Christians have ever experienced and, unfortunately, have had drummed into their heads: "This is *the* group; leave this work, and you leave God." Well, they start believing that is true. They actually fear and believe God has left them because they left *the* work of God.

(Just about every group has —it seems—one of those awful stories to tell about someone who left the movement and shortly thereafter died. I wonder if it ever occured to them that a few people *inside* the movement had also died! Anyway, the use of fear of any kind is a sure sign of deep insecurity on the part of the leaders. Using fear tactics and death stories doesn't point to either self-confidence nor God-confidence in a worker.)

I wish Christians would stop telling those stories. There must be a dozen movements claiming to be "it" . . . and all of them with a "he left and then died" story. The only possible conclusions I can reach based on this scenario are either God has a dozen movements, each of which is "*the* work of God in this generation," and you'll have some awful curse fall on you if you leave any one of the dozen, or somebody is using scare tactics to keep their membership from walking out on them!

What happens to the Christian who has heard all these stories, yet one day knows he has to leave the movement for conscience's sake? Or sanity's sake? Trauma sets in. There is uncertainty. For sure, the group doesn't make leaving easy. A guilt trip *par excellence* seems to accompany leaving.

When I hear the stories of the authoritarian oppression individuals experienced in these groups, I am amazed to see these dear Christians still in desperate fear "because I left *the* work of God."

Secondly, damaged people who have left these movements are so distrusting of any Christian groups—anywhere—I sometimes wonder whether they will trust the Lord's return. Consequently, it is difficult to point a damaged Christian to something that is better. He cannot see anything as holding hope for him.

What can I say? This. "Listen, Christian. Listen, Ken. You have been subject to an appeal to your pride and also to fear tactics. The appeal to your pride was to get you into a movement and committed to that movement. The fear tactics kept you in, even when you wanted to leave. (Those are methods so ancient they creak.) That group—as glorious as it was—was not the only work of the Lord on earth. Somewhere, Christians have something better and deeper. The Lord did not leave you.

Furthermore, that emptiness, that pain is something that you—and you alone—have done to yourself. And you, and you alone, *can* break loose. You *can* break that morbid cycle which you put yourself into.

5

Dear Ken:

I watched the release of *A Tale of Three Kings* with a great deal of interest. Besides those who think it's a Christmas story(!), there are others who read the book and seem to think that I am taking a stand on their side of the issue of authoritarianism. And it doesn't matter which side they are on, they nonetheless see the book being on *their* side.

Of course, there are a few who do not share that outlook. One minister publicly forbade his followers to read the book. (Good! At least we've identified one authoritarian.)

Well, what is my view? For the record, I am very opposed to Christian leaders telling people how to live their private lives. I find no basis for this in the New Testament.

Here are a few weather vanes to watch in assessing authoritarianism in a group.

INSISTENCE ON LIVING IN COMMON

I once had the experience of living in common with a group of very dear and wonderful people. This experience lasted for three years. I want you to know, Ken, that it was hard. It was also wonderful. It was both a sweet memory and, at times, a nightmare. There were about one hundred of us in the experiment and, as far as I know, without exception we were deeply grateful for that experience. We also heaved a sigh of relief when it was over! I think I can speak for most of those who went through that three-year experience by saying, "It was great, but it should not become a life-long way of living. Every Christian ought to have a go at it, but it is not to be recommended as a thirty-year-long lifestyle." I do especially recommend it for the unmarried. The married? On the *long* haul, there are more dangers to a marriage in living in common than there are benefits.

To this day, I still urge singles to live in common. It's a wonderful experience, and virtually all seem to enjoy it. But for others, I would not recommend it for more than six months or a year. Two years on the outside and that is stretching it! Further, I would hope that some very compassionate person(s)—who has had previous experience in living in common—would be around to give a great deal of very compassionate help, counsel, and guidance to any couple trying this experience even for a weekend!

In retrospect, living in common was something that seemed to have been more difficult upon wives than upon husbands. I think that is something very important to note and to be aware of before going into it.

I would like no one to think that I am opposed to living in common; but for the married I am for it only under the most ideal circumstances.

Now, why have I brought up the subject of living in common? For this reason: Authoritarian groups often live in common—or at least in community. I think there are reasons other than Scriptural ones that often cause leaders of authoritarian groups to take on this lifestyle as a permanent thing. I repeat, I think the reasons may have nothing to do with Scripture. The reasons may be found in the psychological flaws of the leader's nature. I'll come to that in a moment.

But let me say now, living in common in authoritarian groups is often begun—wittingly or unwittingly—for the purpose of control. Let me tell you a little bit about our own experiences. As I look back upon the experience of living in common I first remember that no group of people ever went into anything so naively. We started off living in community, and that was an experience that had always been wonderful. And so, the Christians within the fellowship wanted to go the full distance. Some of us, including myself, were very reluctant. As we got into living in common, we found ourselves changing things radically every few months. Why? Because nothing worked! Little by little it dawned on us that we had a mammoth project underway that none of us had been prepared for. During the three years we lived in common, we tamed most of our problems, but some we never resolved (such as how to keep automobiles running or how to get people to remember to pick us up from work at 5 o'clock if they were running!)

Fortunately, we were doing this prior to the rise of the present-day authoritarian movement. I look back now and make a few observations in the light of what's happened in our country since that time. I am grateful we were a free people. (Sometimes "free-for-all" might have been a better word!) There was no one among us who had the psychological need to control other people's lives. Secondly, nearly everything we did, of any major consequence, was decided in open meetings and *not* in small closed meetings. You might be interested to know that we had no elders and no one among us had even heard anything (of consequence) about submission and authority.

There was a natural feeling among all of us that we were in this thing together, and by mutual agreement we were going to muddle our way through it. Further, no one had to live in common if they didn't want to. In the beginning, almost all did. But later some elected not to. Perhaps the most telling point here is that those who did not live in common were not looked down upon. (No one even thought in those terms—and if some of us did, we should not have.)

I learned a great deal about living in common, just as I have learned a great deal about living in community. When I think of the practice of living in common in the hands of men who are inclined to control other people's lives, I shudder. What a potentially powerful tool living in common could become in the hands of Christian authoritarians.

What do I mean? Well, take a man who does not hesitate to scare people out of their wits with two of the most powerful tools known to humanity. If you don't know what those two tools are, one of them is Scripture and the other one is God. When you threaten people with a Scriptural view of something and then tell them it will please (or displease) God, and add to that a situation in which all money is controlled by one individual or a small group, you have some very powerful tools in your hands. Even further, add to that the ingredient of total conformity by everyone to one set of morals, one set of social standards, and one set of clothing and you have a situation that is not only potentially harmful to brothers and sisters, you have a situation that probably cannot be justified from even the most extreme view of Scripture.

Maybe I should comment on that last statement. The Paulinian churches obviously did not live in common. We cannot even say that the churches in Judea nor the churches in Jerusalem lived in common on a permanent basis. But never in the history of the early Church, in my judgment, was control exercised to the extent that it is sometimes exercised in some authoritarian movements today.

The thought of mixing together living in common and authoritarianism is a scary thought indeed. But Ken, the big problem that faces you is not something your group is doing. Here is the heart of the problem: Are you involved in something that has origins in God or origins primarily in one man's psychological need to control others? That question cannot be dogmatically answered by anyone this side of heaven. At the very, very best, each of us must follow what we individually believe to be the Lord's own word to us.

It is not the approach nor the method, but it is the *man* that decides the spirit and atmosphere of a movement. Consequently, I could never oppose nor bless any method nor any approach of any sane Christian group. It is the man, not the practice, that will ultimately harm or bless God's people.

Perhaps living in common could be harmless and a wonderful experience in good and wise hands. I don't know.

I hope that you will keep in mind, then, that whatever your conclusion is about the movement that you've been in, remember that there is a 50-50 chance that you may be wrong. I simply do not know of any permanent guidelines by which we can judge all groups and all movements as to whether they are "good" or "bad." Certainly, the practice of living in common can be potentially harmful to an awful lot of Christians, if it is carried out in an atmosphere of oppression.

THE TREATMENT OF WOMEN

Let me tell you a story. When I was a very young minister, I had a radio program. It was a 15-minute devotional program. Right after me was a Pentecostal evangelist. He always came in dressed like Rockefeller. Tripping in behind him was this pale-faced wife clothed in the latest flour sack creations! That happened to be the stage Pentecostalism was in in that day. Today, in the Pentecostal movement, women seem to dress about as nicely as their husbands do. So, things have changed in Pentecostalism. But the practice of dressing women in burlap is still going on in other groups.

There has been a lot of emphasis in the authoritarian movements on dress. Many of these movements are putting their women back in the medieval age. But that is not what troubles me. What troubles me is the position women hold within the movement. I would repeat, the major crush of authoritarianism seems to fall more on women than it does on men.

A couple came to visit us from just such a movement. They had planned to be with us for a few weeks. As soon as they arrived, the wife announced that she was leaving the movement and she was also leaving her husband unless he left that movement. Something had snapped inside of her. It had to do with having tasted freedom again.

Now perhaps this is an extreme example, but I nonetheless have the impression that, in general, men fare far better in authoritarian movements than do women.

A very wise Christian worker (who happened to be a woman) once said to me that you can ususally tell just how authoritarian a movement is by the degree to which head covering is pushed within the movement. I found that an extremely interesting observation. (I would only add that that does not necessarily mean physical head covering, but rather, the whole subject of covering as it relates to authority.)

Anyway, the place of women in a movement is a second possible clue by which a person might be able to better understand whether or not the group he is in is perhaps a group he should not be in. Another is...

THE POWER OF ELDERS

None of us would dispute that the Scripture teaches us to submit "to those whom the Lord has placed over us." Now the question is: Submit how much and where? The second question is: Did the Lord place those elders over me? Or, did some man place men (who are called elders) over me?

Look at it this way. I work for a living. I am a school teacher. My principal has a certain control over my life, and yet that control has very definite limits. If he presses beyond those limits, there is something very, very wrong going on in that school. No, not in the school, but in the man. The local government in the city I live in has control over me. So does the federal government, but those controls are limited. If those controls become all inclusive, I am no longer in a democracy nor a republic but in an authoritarian state. So the question must be asked: When God put elders within the church to exercise some amount of direction, just how much control did He allow those elders to exercise in your personal, private life? Surely, there must be limits.

Let's turn that question around.

Whenever the Scripture comments on something, it usually does so in two ways. First, by an out and out statement. (In the New Testament the *statements* are usually found in the Epistles and are void of illustrations.) The Scripture also usually *illustrates* the statements that it makes. (The Gospels and Acts usually give us the illustrations.)

Now, then, run through your mind all the illustrations of elders and apostles exercising control over God's people, as recorded in Scripture. Can you think of any? Even Peter, in those early and crisis days of the church in Jerusalem, made the clear comment that Ananias and Sapphira could have kept all their money and property. (Point: Doing what everyone else was doing was *not* mandatory.) Their sin was not in what they kept, but in their lying.

My point is this; I find no illustrations in the New Testament that are even remotely similar to the control being exercised by "elders" over God's people in authoritarian groups. Any illustrations the Scripture presents of the authority of elders over our lives seem to be—at best—very narrow and very, very limited.

THE TEN YEAR TEST

I am sharing with you some of my convictions, but I am also sharing with you some yardsticks by which you might be able to decide in your own mind what you should do. Therefore, I shall venture another suggestion. If a movement is ten years old, you can tell a lot more about it than when it is two years old. All works look good when they are one or two years old. Here's a good question to ask of a movement that is a decade old: Just how many ex-elders are there?

Let me illustrate what I mean. A man begins a movement. In some solemn ceremony, he ordains a group of elders and announces to God's awaiting people that these men have been chosen by God and appointed by God to have authority over them. Well, a few years pass and some of those elders defy—or at least disagree with—the founder. (You can be sure some will also side with him.)

The leader gets upset and announces that those who've opposed him are men who are of the devil. He throws them out—or in some ugly scene—they leave. He now sets about ordaining new elders whom God has appointed over the Lord's people. Eventually, some of these also disagree with him, there is a split, the whole thing is of the devil, etc., etc.

Now Ken, it is obvious that something is wrong in a scenario like this. How can men be elders one year and of the devil the next year? How is it that I give my life utterly to a man (an elder)—to control my life—one year, and the next year he is denouncing the man who ordained him (and vice versa)?

I am reluctant to use an illustration like this because I believe such a thing could have happened even in the New Testament, on occasion. But when something like this becomes a consistent pattern, then I raise a red flag of danger in measuring that movement.

THE LEADER'S REACTION UNDER PRESSURE

Every man in leadership in the Kingdom of God gets under pressure. There's not a one of us who comes through that 100% perfect. The pressures come. They rise to unbearable heights, then recede. Soon they will rise, and they will recede again. We get most of our work done when there's not a whole lot of pressure; and we get more of our transformation when there is.

Every Christian worker has certain weaknesses, failures, and inabilities, so you can't hang a man for that. But here is a good yardstick of a man's internal spiritual strength: When his work is under attack, when pressure has mounted, when a split threatens his work, how does he react?

Is the worker *consistently* defensive? Does he blame a lot of things on the devil? Does he show hostility? Does he show bitterness? Do these attitudes and thoughts begin creeping into his *public ministry*? Does he start making oblique references to certain mysterious events that everyone listening understands as being reference to people who have hurt his work?

(By the way, if he is someone who publicly, consistently attacks people around him or people in his past or in the present—if it is a consistent trait of his, year after year—then I would recommend that you leave that movement immediately. There is something seriously wrong with it... no, him.)

You can tell a great deal about a work when it gets under pressure. It is my observation that when a man does a great deal of lashing out at others and of defending himself, that man is showing that he is quite insecure and even unsure of himself and his work. I would also say, in at least a good number of cases, it is just such men who tend to foster movements in which they exercise a great deal of control. Regardless of outward appearances, men who exercise a lot of control over other people's lives are basically very insecure people, uncertain of their call and sending from God.

I would also add this question for you to consider. At the end of ten years, just how many people have been excommunicated from the movement? (Sometimes they're not excommuniated, but perhaps they are pressured out by the group, or they are counseled to leave, or they are shown they are not welcome.) If a lot of people have left your movement in *that* way, then I would say you were in a situation that is Scripturally inordinate.

I hasten to say that large numbers of people usually go tripping in the front door and out the back door of most Christian movements. The question is not the numbers that come and go. The question is: Were they thrown out? Was their leaving an ugly thing? Or did they encounter true Christian grace, understanding and love as they struggled through the question of whether or not to leave?

I think I would add a terribly important question: Of the people who left, how many of them feel really comfortable in coming back to the group for a visit? The answer to that simple little question may hold more guidelines in it than anything else I have written in these letters. How would you be treated if—having left— you returned to visit?

HOW MUCH CONTROL?

If you are in a movement in which people are told whom to

marry or whom to divorce, if you are in a group that gets *that* far into people's personal lives, then I would recommend that you get out immediately for you are not only in an authoritarian movement, you are in a potentially dangerous movement.

EXCLUSIVENESS

Just how exclusive is your group's view of the church? If it does not recognize all other evangelicals as believers and part of the family of the faith, then, again, you are in a very questionable situation. Another thing to ask yourself: Does your movement perceive different levels of Christians? Such appeals go straight to a Christian's ego. ("We are overcomers." "We are the covenant keepers." "We will reign with Christ." "Others are doing fairly well." "Others are backsliders." "Those who do not follow us are in big trouble with God.") Any group that categorizes some Christians as being special to God as over against others, well, I would say: here is yet another red flag. A danger signal.

THE PSYCHOLOGICAL MAKEUP OF YOUR LEADER

I discuss this subject with fear and trembling because I realize there are a lot of really good Christian men in this world who have enemies and those enemies will use anything they can find to use against them.

I would like to repeat that Absaloms are just as dangerous as supposed Sauls. Therefore, with great reluctance, I ask this question and would like for you to remember that in itself it is not crucial. But if it fits into an overall mosaic, it becomes very crucial.

Here's the question: Does the man who is leading the movement have in his nature a need to control everyone within his environment?

There are people who have this psychological flaw: the need to control. Sometimes the Lord breaks that in a man's life and only the residue of it is seen. The Lord can use a man who has had this problem in his life, just as He can use a man who despises being a leader but who—nonetheless—is made a leader by the Lord. But, if this need to control remains unbroken in a man, then he will almost always tend towards authoritarianism. Sometimes this trait surfaces in the beginnings of a work, sometimes in the middle, and sometimes it takes many, many years for this problem to come out into the light.

As I said, I am very reluctant to include this question because there are a lot of strong men who serve the Lord and serve Him well and have good reason under God for what they do.

GROUP CONFORMITY

Within every group that has ever been known to man since the dawn of history, there has been group conformity. It may be the U.S. Marines or it may be a kindergarten Sunday School class. It could be the Cult of the Purple Hand, or it could be the Cub Scouts. If you are part of a group, there is group pressure—even by accident. So my question is not: Is there group pressure? Of course there is group pressure. The question is: Is that group pressure encouraged? Is it fed? And beyond that, is group pressure deliberately and frequently used to control the lives of others?

* * * *

I end the list here. Remember, those are—at best—guiding questions every person must answer *wholly* for himself. A man may try to build a case if he sees in the above list some of the attributes of the movement he is in. But I doubt if you have a case if only one or two of these danger signals exist. But if they are all there and if they are all screaming loud and clear, if red flags are flying all over the place, well then I think you might be wise to consult the local bus schedule for the earliest departure time.

Oh yes, I would like to repeat something I said in *A Tale of Three Kings.* Get hold of a boxful of books entitled "Animal Farm," pass them out to all your friends within your movement... to the elders, to the leaders. Ask absolutely everyone to read the book. If the people within your movement can read that book and survive, then I don't think you are in an authoritarian movement.

I would like to say that I once had the privilege of distributing *Animal Farm* to every Christian with whom I fellowshipped. There wasn't so much as a trickle upon the face of the waters. I shall never forget the comment of one dear Christian woman: "My goodness, I never realized how awful communism was until I read that book." Brother, if the people you live with and love can read that book and have nothing more to say than something like that, then there is a possibility you are in good hands.

I'll go a little further. I doubt that any authoritarian group that allowed all of its members to read that book could survive wholly intact. I'll go further still...I believe it would be wise for the leadership of any group that was concerned that it might evolve into an authoritarian group to have everyone within their movement read that book. I think it would be one of the healthiest things that a group of Christians could do.

I'll go further still...I dare the leaders of authoritarian Christian groups to read that book and pass it out to their people.

With that I close.

6

Dear Ken:

I think I would like to make an observation on a comment often made by men about checks and balances within a movement.

I notice that men who head up authoritarian groups (and, to be fair, this is an observation often made in non-authoritarian groups, too) state that a plurality of elders is a protection on God's people from being led into something that is harmful. The point being that a plurality of eldership serves as a check and balance. On the other hand, they maintain, a movement that is headed by one man is much more susceptible to fallacy. That certainly looks good on the surface.

Nonetheless, I question the hypothesis. First, it's impossible for one man to run any movement. He has to have help. It is inherent, then, that he would have influence over the people around him. It is perfectly easy for a man to identify those whom he influences, give them labels (elder, deacon, etc.) and then announce that there is a plurality of leadership and, therefore, there are checks and balances. That ain't necessarily so.

I recall no movement in church history (at least none that made a lasting contribution to the history of God's people) but what that movement began under the dynamic leadership of just one man or one woman. My point is this: any new Christian movement will almost certainly be founded by one central figure. It does not follow that monolithic leadership or multi-leadership is any indication of which direction that movement will go. When a movement is young, there is one man up there somewhere who leads; others follow.

The heart of the matter is not whether there are checks and balances and whether or not there is plurality of leadership or one-man rule, or even democracy. Any of those can turn out to be a horror... or any of them can turn out to be something beautiful.

It is not difficult to find groups that are greatly blessed who have one Christian in control. There are groups like that all over the world and some of them have the respect of Christians in all the major evangelical movements. The same is true of a movement, usually much older, in which there is a true plurality of leadership. You can just as easily find groups that are led by one man, which are a disaster, and groups that boast of a plurality of leadership that are also a disaster.

Ken, there is no such thing as a method, system, or structure which can guarantee the protection and safety of God's people. In fact, they have virtually nothing to do with how God's people will fare in *any* movement.

What a group of Christians will be, what a group of Christian people are, what that movement will eventually become, has little to do with either doctrine, organizational set-up, or the method by which they work. A movement's destiny is found in one place and in one place only, and that is in the hidden recesses of the heart of the man who leads that group. For better or for worse, it is the hidden motives of his heart that dictate what that movement will become.

If a tyrant lurks within that man's heart, that group will eventually know tyranny. If that man has within him a broken heart, a compassionate spirit, a shattered will... well, the people will probably be rather safe.

(Another major factor will be *what is going on in the hidden parts of the hearts of those who are following him!*)

Ken, it is the heart, it is the motives, it's the goals, it's t⊦ psychological makeup of the leader that dictate the direction of the movement and the safety or danger in which God's people live. Doctrines and teachings account for very little. The doctrines and practices most emphasized will at best reflect the psychological makeup of the man.

(I would like for you to know that I believe that if a man has been truly dealt with by the Lord, his doctrines and teachings will not generally reflect his own nature, but will truly, genuinely reflect what the true and Living God is really like.)

It is the brokenness or the lack of it, it is the awesome spiritual depth or the lack of that depth, that are the unseen navigators of any movement.

It is an unfortunate fact that no one has yet invented a Geiger counter which we can place over a man's heart and get a good read-out of what he is really like inside. Time and time alone can accomplish that.

And it usually takes ten to twelve years to really find out.

* * * *

Then, what is your choice, Ken? Your choice is whether to gamble or not to gamble. Are you willing?

Let us take a young man who is 22 years old. Here is a young man who wants to become part of something that God is truly the author of. At some point he will have to gamble on a man and a movement. No matter what that movement is, no matter what the man says, what that young Christian is gambling is ten to twelve years of his life. Ten or twelve years pass and he is now 32 or 34; he should pretty well know what kind of a movement he has joined. He may now be faced with making his decision all over again.

In your case, Ken, you have to decide whether or not your gamble paid off. Did you become part of a really wonderful work of

God? If the answer is "yes," then I suppose you want to continue with that people. But if your gamble turned sour, you have some new choices to make. If you feel that gambling ten years of your life was a mistake, then you should probably leave that group.

But Ken, here's the real rub. If you feel that you have "wasted" twelve years of your life, will the fact that you gambled and (apparently) lost, destroy your life?

Ken, it was you who gambled. *You* made the choice. Ken, it is you who must bear responsibility. If it was a bad decision, you really have no one to blame but yourself.

I believe the Christian who has joined the worst possible group, if he gets out of it, should take what he learned and treat the lessons he learned as gold. He should believe those lessons came directly from God, that the Lord had a beautiful purpose in his being part of that ugly thing. He should turn away believing that he has learned valuable lessons, that the Lord has, and can, use those lessons to transform his life. Ken, if you cannot look upon your experience over the past years with those eyes, then you really are in trouble. More trouble than anything that group ever poured on you.

If you are disappointed in that movement, if it is literally destroying your life, there just might be something going on here that is deeper than just a young twenty-year old man giving his life to a movement. (Temporary disillusionment caused by a group is one thing. Permanent destruction bespeaks something entirely different. Frankly, brother, I think if that is what has happened to you, then you probably would never have made it in a much safer movement.) The man who gets embittered has something wrong with his heart. Ken, there is absolutely nothing that should make you bitter. Absolutely nothing. So, I would say to you or to any Christian who has joined a movement and feels that that movement is not of the Lord, that Christian needs to examine his heart very carefully. What were *your* own secret, inner motives for joining that movement? What were your ambitions? What was really in your heart that you did not allow your mind to hear. What *really* disappointed you? Was it that the movement wasn't of God and now you'll never get to be king somebody, as you had secretly hoped?

Are you bitter because of that? Ken, remember, it is not just leaders who are susceptible to rotten hearts and ulterior motives. This is a two-way street.

Ken, I am for you. Don't sit around with bitter people who will spend the rest of their lives doing an anatomy on "what went wrong." Don't sit around conjuring up a theoretical way to have a movement that doesn't make the mistakes of past movements. I repeat, Ken, it is not the doctrine nor the method of that movement, it is the amount of work God has done in the hearts of those who lead that dictates the future of any work.

By the way, Ken, if later in your life you ever try leading a group of people, I can almost guarantee that within six months of the beginning you are going to go through one of the greatest rearrangements of theology that a man can possibly know . . . not to mention the crash-course in humility that you are going to receive. For sure you are going to be sorely tempted to do some of the very things you now despise.

The failures that we have seen in our land over the last few decades have come about because men's hearts and because of poor preparation. Bitterness has come, not from injustices that have happened to Christians, but from the heart's inability to accept those hardships and to surrender those tragic years to the Lord. Unless your heart clears up, given similar conditions to those your former leaders had over you, you would commit similar sins.

Thank Him for what you have been through. Walk away rejoicing . . . believing that those things were put into your life by the sovereign hand of God. For *your* benefit.

7

Dear Ken:

Perhaps I am coming to the very heart of the matter.

Each of us have to follow our inner sense of the Lord who dwells within us.

You've come from a movement that taught people to "consult your covering." Now, how did anyone get that out of Scripture? On the other hand, I have to remember that you agreed to that arrangement when you became part of the work, and so did hundreds like you.

I do not need to tell you that it is always easier to have someone else announce what the will of God is for your life than it is for you to find it out on your own.

I share with you my own experience of the last thirty years. The will of God has not always been easily known in my life. I have often found myself having to wait. Wait a *long* time—much longer than I wished—to know His will. I have tried to listen to His voice, only to hear the resounding roars of utter silence. But most of all I have had to cut through a thousand hidden motives of my heart. I have had to deal with all the logical thought processes that have come into this damaged and fallen thing called my intellect. I have had to thread my way through the specters of hundreds of my own ambitions. I have had to grope about, seeking some way—how, I cannot say—to enter into my spirit and there to wait, and eventually to understand, and finally to obey.

The Lord planted something deep within you, Ken. Your spirit is the highest counsel in the universe. Never allow that counsel to abdicate to any other counsel. No, not to another man's will. And Ken, *not* to *your* own will, either. Somewhere deep within your spirit is the will of God.

Ken, cut past the thunderous cries of your own terribly logical logic. Get past your feelings. Get past your desires and your reasonings, and find your God again. The highest Court in the universe is still inside you. Listen. Eventually, you will hear. Then, obey. Him.

8

Dear Ken:

You will have to break away from the devastation in your life. You alone can do it. You are going to have to erase the past. What you have gone through must be dealt with; otherwise, you are going to be worthless to the Lord, to His Kingdom. And, if your situation is really bad, you are going to be almost worthless to society.

You may not like this letter.

Let me tell you something that really isn't pleasant to share. I have a friend. About seventeen years ago he became part of a brand new Christian movement. He was in the movement for 12 or 13 years before he finally had to break with it. During that period the movement went through many changes, evolving from being something that was seeking to be pure to becoming almost a duplicate of the religious system . . . the very thing that movement was supposed to be against. When this brother left the movement, the church he was with also pulled out with him.

I am telling you this story because of a conversation I had with him. During that period when he left, a lot of other Christians left that same movement. Almost all of those Christians are virtually destroyed. Some of those devastated Christians moved to the city where my friend lives. They became part of the church fellowship he led. They were hunting for a home; they were hunting for a harbor; they were hunting for peace; they were hunting for a place to get well. I asked that dear brother, "What are those people like today?"

He was candid with his answer. He said, "Virtually every person who has come to us from out of that movement is inflicting great damage to our church." I inquired as to what he meant, although I thought I knew.

One attribute of these people was: they talked about the past all the time. They talked about it in front of anyone. I don't think they realized, and I speak for myself, that we don't really want to hear those ghastly stories! We weren't there; we don't like to hear criticism of other Christians no matter how much the person telling the story thinks the other fellow was in the wrong. The rest of us simply are not interested in subjecting our inner man to so much negativity.

A second characteristic of those folks was that they were always warning the young people in his church to be very, very careful. About what? Almost anything. The list goes on and on forever. People who leave movements seem to be filled with fear and seem to need to caution all the rest of the Christians in the world to be careful about everything. We cannot live our lives being *that* cautious. We do not wish to live in fear. We still have the heart to dare and we still have the heart to trust.

That was another thing he told me. Those kinds of Christians do not trust anyone. Especially, they do not trust Christian workers. They cannot believe that there is an honest man out there anywhere. That is really tragic. When a person has reached that point, his life as a Christian has been destroyed.

My friend shared with me that he, too, was always being counselled to be careful here, and to be careful there. Those who had left the movement were filled with all sorts of theories and philosophies about what should never be done and about what should always be done.

Another attribute of the folks who had left that movement was their fear of elders, their fear of leaders, their fear of any kind of leadership. Usually, their concept of the church had boiled down to something so ethereal that if tried on a practical basis, a church would probably never be able to get together even for a first meeting!

Another attribute was that they tended to run around with one another, constantly filling one another's garbage pail with new garbage—or should I say, with old garbage.

Perhaps the most tragic thing of all was that these very Christians who had been hurt by authority and by division were themselves now causing a split within the church fellowship of my friend! How tragic.

Cynical, fearful, almost paranoid. And now even divisive. Ken, is this what you want to end up being as a Christian?

I know what your response may be. "But I have been hurt by other Christians so deeply." Ken, that simply is not true. No one in the world has hurt you . . . (unless they laid you down on a torture rack and stuck you with a hot poker!) No, you have not been hurt by anyone. Only one person can hurt you and that person is you. Every pain you've known, you have inflicted upon yourself. One of the foundations of human survival is to understand this simple point: "It is not what men do to you but how you react to what men do to you that determines how you will survive and live upon this planet."

Ken, you have but one person in this world to indict for any attitudes of bitterness, cynicism, hurt or pain. That person is yourself and it lies within your jurisdiction, and yours alone, to decide whether or not you wish to continue the patterns that are beginning to be set in your life, or whether you wish to break from them and head for the sunlit meadows of higher ground.

I have one more letter to write you, Ken. In it I will share with you my deepest feelings on this matter of devastation.

9

Dear Ken:

This letter is about a very practical matter: How can you get past devastation?

Is it possible to get past devastation? Can a Christian overcome bitterness? First of all, I would like to say that those are fearful questions. Many brothers and sisters cannot pull free of bitterness once they have bit into that fruit.

I would like to give you some guidelines on what to do with your life in relationship to a movement you feel has destroyed you.

First of all, you need to search your own heart and realize that a great deal of the problem lies within your own psychological makeup. There are people who have been mistreated worse than you, who have not been hurt as deeply as you. Some not at all. I think there is a strong possibility that Christians who get hurt in authoritarian movements have a weakness toward cynicism, bitterness, and criticism, anyway. Or perhaps, they walked into that situation with inordinate pride. Ken, you need to remember that you fell for the appeal that "you are special." You got exalted in that. It fed something within your nature. You believed it was the only movement on earth and you told people so. Very often that's a reflection of a person's own psychological problems and you need to face that possibility. Ken, I think a large portion of your problem and that of every brother and sister who has been hurt by these groups is that you feel like you have been sold a bill of goods. I will not argue that point. But remember, that bill of goods appealed to you.

Perhaps the thing that troubles me more deeply than anything else is that, as I see those who have been so deeply hurt, they seem to be totally unwilling to turn to the Lord for a way out. It is almost as though they are not only angry with the movement; they are also angry with God. Is this true of you?

Have you turned to the Lord for total deliverance from the dark emotions you are feeling?

For some, it is almost as though they feel it was God who sold them a bill of goods. I find many Christians damaged by authoritarianism almost totally incapable of seeing the hand of God in their past experience. Until that moment does come, there simply is no hope for a devastated Christian. The fact that a Christian will not allow himself to see that horrible nightmare as something that had purpose in it from the viewpoint of God is, in itself, an indication that that Christian has something very, very wrong with the inward motives of his own life.

Ken, I have been even-handed in my assessment of authoritarianism. I am personally and privately opposed to this whole present-day concept. But I have also spent a good part of the last thirty years of my ministry counselling Christians. During that time, you cannot help but begin to have some kind of insight into human nature.

A great deal of the devastation I see in Christians coming out of these movements simply need not happen. God did not so construct human nature as to forever fall apart just because they had five or ten years at the hands of unscrupulous men. There is no reason for a Christian going on in bitterness throughout his whole life. The problem cannot be laid at the feet of those who were the authoritarians. A problem that goes on that long has to be dealt with. Ken, you need the Lord and you need Him desperately.

With that introduction, I would like to give you a few guidelines to consider.

First of all, if you have been talking about this experience to other Christians almost incessantly, then I would say to you it's time to stop. I have seen Christians who cannot stop talking about it. You meet them; they are perfect strangers and in three minutes they are telling you their whole nightmarish story. An hour later they are telling someone else. I would say, keep your mouth closed. With it, I would make some resolutions, if I were you. Resolve to never refer to the incident again, no matter how long you live. And that is even if it means you have to stop referring to a twelve or fifteen year period of your life. I would add to that, never use it as an example in any of your public ministry. In other words, stop talking about it utterly and totally.

On the other hand, if you happen to be one of those Christians who bottles things up and never says anything and you have never talked about it, then it is time you sat down and had a long talk with someone and got it out of your system. (For goodness sake don't select me, I've heard too much already!)

This next suggestion is not going to go over very well, I am sure. I am keenly aware that those of us who live outside of formal and structured Christianity generally have some pretty strong convictions against counselors and psychologists. Nonetheless, Ken, when a man's mind has been dealt a blow this great, I would seriously recommend that you find a professional Christian counselor and have four or five sessions with him. This is so that you can get this thing talked out once and for all. But more than that, if he is an insightful Christian counselor, he might help you come up with some personal problems of your own that you may not be aware of.

I am going to repeat this. Ken, there may be unknown reasons why you have been so devastated by this. Again, I am awed by the number of Christians who find it utterly impossible to take this experience as from the hand of God . . . something that He meted out to them because He loved them, that this experience had divine purpose.

The next statement will also sound very unusual, coming

from someone like me. I think you should consider going back to organized Christianity. If you cannot handle the experience you've gone through, there is no need for you to sit out here in the wilderness until your bones bleach in the sand. You can at least go to Sunday morning church meetings in a church building and hear messages of comfort and faith and strength. If you cannot totally get healed, I do not think that it is healthy for you to sit around forever, licking you wounds.

There are good things to be said for structured Christianity. There is comfort and solace to be found in some places within structured Christianity. I recommend that if you cannot pull totally free of this devastation, then consider returning to some sort of denominational movement where you can get some help and comfort, be it ever so mild.

I would like to repeat: Stop running around with the people who have come out of that movement that you were in. I find in talking with Christians who have come out of these movements, it's like the clock stopped—there is nothing new in their lives, there is nothing healthy; and all of their friends are ex-members of that movement. This is not healthy; it should be stopped.

Next Ken, you are going to have to start believing. You are going to have to start believing there are decent and honest workers out there. You are going to have to believe that there *are* movements born of God. You are going to have to believe that there are movements on this earth—either now or yet to be born—better than the work that you were in. You are going to have to trust Christians and workers again.

Some way, Ken, this thing has got to be broken in you. If you have to, go on a fast. If you have to, then set aside an hour every day to pray and fight this thing out before the throne of God. Tell Him you want to be delivered and you want your mind to stop feeding on past memories. Get down on your knees, down on your face, and tell the Lord you mean to pull free; that you mean to be restored. Don't turn Him loose until He has made you whole again—in your heart and in your mental processes.

Start looking for an encounter with God. You need a miracle; ask for one. A moment of deliverance from past memories.

Most of all, Ken, believe that a loving God sent those years into your life...that He had purpose in your being there. *Positive* purpose that can and will glorify him and bless His church. Tell Him you want *that* view. Take that view, for it is the one, the only true way to behold those years. Wasted? Not at all. They came from God. Get a hold on that, and one day you will bless him for those years.

In those hands,
Gene

FOOTNOTES

[1]Any movement has basically three ways it can grow: 1) through evangelizing the lost, 2) reaching the individual Christian seeker, and 3) by something called "courting"—courting a struggling, little independent group. The latter being easiest (the question of ethics aside) it is, therefore, also the most popular method used by movements to increase their number.

[2]The only other one around that is as popular is called "the restoration of the gifts in our generation." Can you believe it? Historically, this call began with those very words during the period of the French Revolution (1790). A call to recover the gifts has worked so effectively for 200 years in building movements that today this method is in use as much as ever.

THE DEEPER CHRISTIAN LIFE

ARE YOU INTERESTED IN READING MORE ABOUT THE DEEPER CHRISTIAN LIFE?

If you are, let us suggest the order in which to read the following books, all of which have been written on the deep aspects of the Christian life.

By all means, begin with *The Divine Romance.* Then we recommend *Experiencing the Depths of Jesus Christ* and *Practicing His Presence.* Follow that with *Final Steps in Christian Maturity* and *The Inward Journey.*

For a study in brokenness, read *A Tale of Three Kings,* a favorite with thousands of believers all over the world.

The book entitled *The Spiritual Guide, Letters of Mme. Guyon* and *Letters of Fenelon,* all help to solidify, expand and buttress the things you will have read in the previous books.

You might also desire to read Guyon's *Study of Exodus, Job, Song of Songs, Revelation,* thereby gaining *her* view of what she referred to as "The Scripture, seen from *the interior way.*"

BOOKS BY MADAME GUYON

EXPERIENCING THE DEPTHS OF JESUS CHRIST

Guyon's first and best known book. One of the most influential pieces of Christian literature ever penned on the deeper Christian life. Among the multitudes of people who have read this book and urged others to read it are: John Wesley, Adoniram Judson, Watchman Nee, Jessee Penn-Lewis, Zinzendorf, and the Quakers. A timeless piece of literature that has been on the "must read" list of Christians for 500 years.

FINAL STEPS IN CHRISTIAN MATURITY

This book could well be called volume two of EXPERIENCING THE DEPTHS OF JESUS CHRIST. Here is a look at the experiences a more advanced and faithful Christian might encounter in his/her walk with the Lord. Without question, next to EXPERIENCING THE DEPTHS, here is Mme. Jeanne Guyon's best book.

UNION WITH GOD

Written as a companion book to EXPERIENCING THE DEPTHS OF JESUS CHRIST, and includes 22 of her poems.

GENESIS

SONG OF SONGS

Jeanne Guyon wrote a commentary on the Bible; here are two of those books. SONG OF SONGS has been popular through the centuries and has greatly influenced several other well-known commentaries on the Song of Songs.

THE SPIRITUAL LETTERS OF MADAME GUYON

Here is spiritual counseling at its very best. There is a Christ-centeredness to Jeanne Guyon's counsel that is rarely, if ever, seen in Christian literature.

THE WAY OUT

A spiritual study of Exodus as seen from "the interior way."

THE BOOK OF JOB

Guyon looks at the life of Job from the view of the deeper Christian life.

CHRIST OUR REVELATION

A profound and spiritual look at the book of Revelation.

BOOKS by Gene Edwards

DIVINE ROMANCE

"How can I go about loving the Lord personally, intimately?" No book ever written will help more in answering this question for you. Not quite allegory, not quite parable, here is the most beautiful story on the love of God you have ever read. Beginning in eternity past, you will see your Lord unfold the only purpose for which He created all things. Plunging into time and space, you behold a breathtaking saga as He pursues His purpose, to have a bride! See His love story through His eyes. Be present at the crucifixion and resurrection as viewed from the heavenly realms. You will read the most glorious and powerful rendition of the crucifixion and resurrection ever described. The story reaches its climax at the end of the ages in a heart-stopping scene of the Lord at last taking His bride unto Himself. When you have finished this book, you will know the centrality of His love for you. A book that can set a flame in your heart to pour out your love upon Him.

A TALE OF THREE KINGS

A book beloved around the world. A dramatically told tale of Saul, David and Absalom, on the subject of brokenness. A book used in the healing of the lives of many Christians who have been devastated by church splits and by injuries suffered at the hands of other Christians.

OUR MISSION

A group of Christian young men in their early twenties met together for a weekend retreat to hear Gene Edwards speak. Unknown to them, they were about to pass through a catastrophic split. These messages were delivered to prepare those young men spiritually for the inevitable disaster facing them. Edwards presents the standard of the first century believers and how those believers walked when passing through similar crises. A remarkable statement on how a Christian is to conduct himself in times of strife, division and crisis. A book every Christian, every minister, every worker will need at one time or another in his life.

THE INWARD JOURNEY
A study in transformation, taking the reader through a journey from time's end to grasp the ways of God in suffering and the cross, and to bring an understanding to why He works the way He does.

LETTERS TO A DEVASTATED CHRISTIAN
Edwards writes a series of letters to a Christian devastated by the authoritarian movement, who has found himself on the edge of bitterness.

CHURCH LIFE
Gene Edwards challenges the lay Christian and minister alike to set aside many of the present day practices of the church and to respond to the growing host of believers who are seeking a living, vital experience of church life. The author calls for the laying down of some of Christendom's most cherished traditions and practices, telling the story of the origin of these traditions and showing that none of them have their roots in first century practice. He then proposes a totally new approach to church planting and church practice, so unique it can only be classified as revolutionary. **Church Life** should not be read by the faint-heared nor by those who are satisfied with the status quo.

PREVENTING A CHURCH SPLIT

This is a study in the anatomy of church splits, what causes them, their root causes, the results, and how to prevent them. A book every Christian will need someday. This book could save your spiritual life, and perhaps that of your fellowship.

CHURCH HISTORY:

These two books bring to bear a whole new perspective on church life.

REVOLUTION, THE STORY OF THE EARLY CHURCH , Vol. 1

This book tells, in a "you are there" approach, what it was like to be a Christian in the first century church, recounting the events from Pentecost to Antioch. By Gene Edwards.

THE TORCH OF THE TESTIMONY

John W. Kennedy tells the little known, almost forgotten, story of evangelical Christians during the dark ages.

CLASSICS ON THE DEEPER CHRISTIAN LIFE:

PRACTICING HIS PRESENCE

The monumental seventeenth century classic by Brother Lawrence, now in modern English. (One of the most read and recommended Christian books of the last 300 years).

The twentieth century missionary, Frank Laubach, while living in the Philippines, sought to put into practice Brother Lawrence's words. Included in this edition are excerpts from Frank Laubach's diary.

THE SPIRITUAL GUIDE

At the time Jeanne Guyon was teaching in the royal court of Louis XIV (in France), a man named Michael Molinos was leading a spiritual revival among the clergy and laymen of Rome! He actually lived in the Vatican, his influence reaching to all Italy and beyond. The great, near great, the unknown sought him out for spiritual counsel. He was the spiritual director of many of the illuminaries of the seventeenth century. He wrote THE SPIRITUAL GUIDE to meet the need of a growing hunger for spiritual direction. The book was, for a time, banned and condemned to be burned. The author was convicted and sentenced to a dungeon after one of the most sensational trials in European history.

Here, in modern English, is that remarkable book.

The following prices are for the year 1988 only; please write for our catalog for price updates and for new releases. All books are paperback unless otherwise noted.

Turkeys & Eagles (Peter Lord) .... 8.95 hb
Autobiography of Jesus Christ .... 8.95 hb
   on cassette tape (6 tape set in album) 29.95
Preventing a Church Split (Edwards) ... 8.95 hb
A Tale of Three Kings (Edwards) 6.95
The Divine Romance (Edwards)(10.95 hb) 7.95 pb
Experiencing the Depths of Jesus Christ (Guyon) 6.95
The Inward Journey (Edwards) 7.95
Letters to a Devastated Christian (Edwards) 4.95
Our Mission (Edwards) 7.95
Revolution, Vol. 1 (Edwards) 6.95
Practicing His Presence (Lawrence, Laubach) 6.95
Union with God (Guyon) 6.95
Final Steps in Christian Maturity (Guyon) .. 6.95
The Spiritual Guide (Molinos) 6.95
Torch of the Testimony (Kennedy) 7.95
Mme. Guyon's Letters 6.95
Fenelon's Letters 6.95
Guyon's Commentaries:
   Genesis 6.95
   Exodus (The Way Out) 6.95
   Song of Songs 6.95
   Job 7.95
   Revelation (Christ, Our Revelation) 7.95

Christian Books Publishing House
The Seedsowers
P.O. Box 3368
Auburn, Maine 04210
207-783-4234
Visa-MasterCard accepted
These books are available through your local Christian book store.